POETRY FOR ANGELS

BY K. L. JOYNER

POETRY FOR ANGELS is a book of poems
Dedicated to the word of God and is inspired
By those words.

No part of this book may be reproduced in any form
Or by any electronic or mechanical means without
Written permission from the author, except for the
Use of brief quotations in a book review.

To Mom,

My biggest fan.

TABLE OF CONTENTS

TABLE OF CONTENTS

AN ANGEL'S TOUCH

I brushed up against something,
Something that I couldn't see,
But it had a warm feel to it,
That ignited everything in me.

I looked around,
And I was all alone,
But a kindling had started,
That I couldn't control.

It burned hotter and hotter,
As my soul screamed.
My heart flooded with love,
And my mind filled with dreams.

Dreams of a life everlasting,
Filled with a paradise never passing.
An though there was no one,
That I could see.

I knew that an angel,
Had bumped into me.

SUDDENLY

Suddenly,
I am free, like never before,
On the wings of an eagle,
High I soar.

Until my eyes have eclipsed the clouds,
And no human is recognized,
When I look down.

Destined for Heaven I think we are,
As I come face to face, with a star.
Leaving behind, all that is life.
LOVE, HATE, MISERY, STRIFE.

Now I see cometh,
Over a beautiful horizon.

The truth of all truths,
The light of all lights.
The face of my Savior,
Is finally in sight.

ECHOES IN THE STORM

Thoughts echo through my mind,
Bringing light to darker times.
Giving me the strength to carry on,
As I fight this vicious storm.

It's a battle that began, long before I was born,
But as a descendant, I must carry on.
Carrying a cross that is too heavy to bear,
I find myself slipping deep into despair.

Just when I feel like I can't go on,
A hand reaches out and calms the storm.
Bringing with it a cleansing light,
That gives me hope, as I continue to fight.

WHO TO BELIEVE

Who to believe,

To the end of time, they try to deceive.

Got us convinced, that want, is a need.

I pray to God, to come and impede,

Asking for His Light, but only darkness is received.

Just like the chances in my life,

Messed off a marriage and a wife.

It was easy, like the roll of the dice.

I thought I was living, but I was frozen, in the ice.

Now, reality unfolds,

I still search for God, but I'm searching in the cold.

My body's numbing, and I'm fearing for my soul,

Then, the Son shines with His Light and I begin to feel alright.

Now comes the melting of the ice,

Or should I say the resurrection of my life?

Thank you, Lord, for believing in me twice.

GLIMPSE OF HEAVEN

Soft drops of rain fell from the sky,

And as I glanced up, one fell into my eye,

And before it could completely dissipate,

I saw a reflection of Heaven's Gate.

The sight of it was something to behold,

As angels greeted people, with chalices of gold.

"Drink and live forever," they said with a smile.

"Because the Lord has blessed you all, every child."

Then the drop of rain that fell into my eye,

Came down my cheek, and I started to cry.

I cried, because as my vision became clear,

I saw that Heaven was no longer near.

THE ENEMY WITHIN

The enemy within,

Is the one that we should fear,

Because he is forever near.

He whispers to us,

Things that are untrue,

And there is nothing,

That he won't do.

He commits sins,

Like raindrops fall,

And in an instant,

He can rationalize it all.

When you look deep inside,

And see as I do.

It's then you'll understand,

That your enemy is you.

You must chase out Satan,

In every, Shape, Substance, and Form.

Then and only then, will your enemy be gone.

DEATH'S LIE (1)

I was a father, with a wife, and a home,

And a little one to call my own.

Now, in just twenty-four hours,

All that has changed.

Now, I'm a lonely man,

With funeral plans to arrange.

With just the turn of a car's wheels,

Across a dotted line.

The treasures of my life,

Are no longer mine.

I can't even begin to control this pain,

And I think it's slowly driving me insane.

Because I've never been the religious type,

But for the first time in my life,

I prayed to God last night.

DEATH'S LIE (2)

For a moment I didn't hear a sound,

Then suddenly, I heard a voice, and it was all around.

It said, "Son hold back your tears and release your pain.

You cry because you're a sinner and you don't understand.

Once you accept Me into your life,

You will smile when you think of your son,

And your wife.

Knowing that they'll never die,

And this thing called death,

Is just a lie."

FOLLOW THE LIGHT

As I leave the comfort of the womb,

I forget about my life in Heaven,

And into evil, I'm consumed.

I scream in pain,

As the sins of man,

Penetrates my veins!

Why O'Lord, am I cursed?

What did I do, to deserve this birth?

Is there any way for me to leave,

And get back to the paradise,

That I once received?

"Of course, my son,"

I heard Him say.

"Just follow my Light,

I'll lead the way."

CONDEMNED

I cry for a soul, that's incomplete,
And for a paradise, it will never meet.

Condemned it was, by itself,
Because, when it searched for blame,
There was no one else.

Convicted of treason, against The Lord,
It sought the riches of Satan,
But found they were a fraud.

I cry now, because I can see,
That the soul, that was condemned,
Belongs to me.

HE'S IN THE CHURCH

The children walked holding hands,

And the sun rose and blessed the land.

The birds were out singing, on limbs they were perched,

Giving thanks to the Lord, in nature's church.

The air was sweet, with the taste of honey,

And the problems of man, all seemed to be funny.

There wasn't a face, that didn't have a smile,

There wasn't a person, not meek as a child.

Visit this place, it's here on Earth,

Just walk right down to your neighborhood church.

You will eat like you're out of control,

Because your soul was starving, when your body was whole,

And the taste of the words that the Lord, puts into your mouth,

Will make you scream, and make you shout.

LORD, LORD, is what you'll say,

And He will hear you every day.

HEAVEN'S LOVE

An angel came down to me,

From the Heavens above,

And said, "Which will it be?

Paradise or love?"

"If I must choose, I will,"

I said to the angel,

"But they're just one in the same,

Isn't love just Heaven by another name?"

Then she vanished,

In a big flash of light,

But before she did.

She said, "Son, you are right."

AGAIN, AND AGAIN (1)

When I was young,

My parents took the time,

To teach me about the Great Devine,

But as I got older, Satan got bolder.

He came to me, as teenage friends,

And I fell for sin, again, and again.

But like all sinners who try to do right.

I prayed for forgiveness, day and night.

So, when Satan came, to claim His prize,

Because I was old and about to demise.

A bright light arose between me and him,

And a figure came forth, deep from within.

Though I sheltered my eyes against the light,

What I could see was a beautiful sight.

AGAIN, AND AGAIN (2)

She didn't speak or make a sound,
But on his knees, the Devil did get down.
Then she spoke, as pretty, as a bird,
But her words, only my soul heard.

"Your life has been a winding road,
But your faith in God has saved your soul."

So, when Satan comes and makes you sin,
Ask of the Lord, He will forgive you,
Again, and again.

MAN'S GOD (1)

Man's God,

Lives on the Earth.

His face is condemning,

And his words are a curse.

But his pockets are lined,

With Earthly gold,

And his pleasures are many,

As they unfold.

So, to those who seek,

The riches of the Earth.

A God is here,

But he's not in the church.

The things he offers,

Are shallow and false,

And in his web of lies,

Souls will be lost.

MAN'S GOD (2)

So, if he comes, and shows his face,

Repent him back to that satanic place.

Because, when The Father comes,

Whose Son is the Lamb.

All souls that are lost,

Will be damned.

I FORGIVE THEM

I forgive a world,

That's turned cold,

And a people with hatred,

Clear to their souls.

In a place such as this,

How can I even try to exist?

They say in time, I to will change,

And the hatred of the world,

Will run through my veins.

But I forgive them,

For what they say,

And how they act, every day.

Because long ago, before I came,

Another took, the entire world's blame,

And in that one sacrificial act,

Humanity was given its life back.

THE BURDEN OF LIFE

If life is a burden that we must bear,

And death is the end of pain and despair.

Then why do I feel a chill in my bones,

When the life of a friend has come and gone.

I should rejoice at their passing,

Their agony in this world,

Is no longer lasting.

But still, we cling to this thing called life,

And fight off death with all our might.

Because, when it comes, then we understand,

That the burdens of life, are the joys of man.

THE WAR FOR HEAVEN

To those who fight,

Against the evils of sin.

Even though you may die,

In the end, you will win.

Though the battle be fought,

Here on Earth,

And the training of soldiers,

Is done in the church.

To the victor, goes eternal life,

And the loser pays a damnable price.

So, now that the battle lines are drawn,

Whose side will you fight on?

IT'S HIS TIME

What are you going to do when he comes for you?

Are you ready?

Is your soul steady?

Are you afraid?

That's okay!

David was too, when the Lord came his way.

Those who say they are not afraid,

Are the ones whose souls will never be raised.

When the Lord comes to lay claim to His flock,

The bravest of men, knees will knock.

As the road to paradise starts to unfold,

And in the Book of Life, names are told.

Many will cry when they don't hear their name,

But, they only have themselves to blame.

PAY NOW OR PAY LATER

What did you do it for?

Did you think you would hear Him roar?

Because you violated His law.

His voice is a whisper,

As low as the floor,

But one you can't ignore.

So, as for you walking out His door,

You'd better think some more.

Now, you can think it's all a game,

And let your violations rein.

But, when it's time to pay them off,

Your soul is exactly what they will cost.

RUNNING WITH THE DEVIL

Running with the Devil,

May seem like fun,

Because the places he stops,

Are the ones God shuns.

So, to those who want,

Their Heaven here on Earth,

The price of admission,

Will be your rebirth.

Into a land,

Where there is no sin,

And beauty is common,

Outside, and in.

So, run if you must,

And enjoy the sights.

But remember, you are running away,

From eternal life.

WHEN SATAN KNOCKS

A messenger of the Devil,

Gave me a call.

He said, "What do you want?

I'll grant it all."

I looked at him,

In his two-thousand-dollar suit,

With his ten-thousand-dollar watch,

And three-thousand-dollar boots.

There I was, in just a pair of old jeans,

With cotton socks on, and tennis shoes,

That needed to be cleaned.

But my head was filled,

With Heavenly thoughts,

And I was walking, The Lord's walk.

Because it's better to bypass,

A few trinkets on Earth.

Then sell your soul, For the price of rebirth.

THE FIGHT FOR ETERNAL LIFE

Parents of the world,

I know your children are your lambs,

But the sins of man cover this land.

So, you must give them,

The weapons they need,

To fight off Satan, when he impedes.

The battle will start,

From the beginning of birth,

And will last, until the day,

They're put to rest in the church.

You must teach them to fight hard,

And to never relinquish their hold.

Because their battle is not for life,

It's for their soul.

THE ANSWER IS THE LIGHT (1)

I questioned myself late one night,

And the answer that I got,

I didn't like.

Why do people have to die?

Why do we have to lie?

To cheat?

To kill?

Are we acting against our will?

These questions to some,

May sound insane,

But after meeting Christ,

Shouldn't we have changed?

Then, the answer appeared, in my head,

And I spoke the words it said.

"You will never see a change,

Because your eyes don't have the range.

THE ANSWER IS THE LIGHT (2)

When you see the Earth,

From God's Heavenly Church,

Then you will see, Christ at work.

He is a beacon, that lights up the night,

But only those souls who are ready,

Can see His Light.

UNTIL TIME ENDS

To the end of time,

That's what He said,

But how can I see it?

If I've longed, been dead.

That's what you get, with the human mind,

Now, let your thoughts, be controlled by the Devine.

He will open your eyes to a beautiful sight,

One that you never would have seen,

Not with all of your Earthly might.

Now, take science and wisdom,

And put them to the side.

Or in the end, you will lose,

Much more than just pride.

GOD'S PEACE

Last night an angel was at the foot of my bed,

I asked her, "What's wrong?

Am I dead?"

She said, "I always come to watch you sleep,

I have never seen a man so at peace.

In a world where sin is all around,

Peace can rarely be found.

There are a few much like yourself,

Who looks towards God,

And nowhere else.

He's the only place to find,

Peace for your, Heart, Soul,

And Mind.

YOU CHOOSE

The angels are singing about marching on,

The Devil's on Earth raging a storm.

Humans are concerned about Earthly wealth,

And putting at risk their eternal self.

Ever since that first bite,

We've been given a choice, between wrong and right.

So, when you choose, try to be bold.

Because you don't choose for yourself,

You choose for your soul.

BELIEVE HIM

The Lord is coming, but we don't know when,

Heaven is a place where there's no sin.

Earth is for those of an Earthly birth,

And facing temptation is how we prove,

Our eternal worth.

The time will come when the test is gone,

And those who have passed will hear the trumpet's horn.

With that sound, there will come a light,

And after that, a beautiful sight.

I say these things because they are true,

Believe in Him, because He believes in you.

READY FOR HEAVEN

Behold the changer of the world,

Be it, Man, Boy, Woman, or Girl.

In the end, it's all the same,

Because it's in the spirit,

Not in the name.

The time is coming upon us fast,

We must act now if we're to last.

Cast your eyes up towards the skies,

To see if the angels are passing by.

To and fro, they go all day,

When they see the Master,

I wonder?

What do they say?

I hope they say that the people of Earth,

Are ready to live, in Your Heavenly Church.

HE'S IN US

The Lord is with us,

As we walk through life.

He's in Sons and Daughters,

And Husbands and Wives

No one exists,

Except by His touch.

No one will ever,

Love us so much.

So, if ever you think,

You need a friend.

Just look inside,

He's deep within.

He will never leave us alone,

We are the ones,

Who run away from home.

FINDING GOD

There are three steps to God,

And they're simple to take.

First, you need to have,

A great deal of faith.

Now, believing in Him is good for a start,

But helping in His work,

Will bring light to your dark.

You will feel Him enter,

And touch your soul.

Now, taste of His Blood,

Like did, The Twelve of Old.

Now that you've found Him,

Grab tight and hold,

But He was never lost,

It was only your soul.

BELIEVE

An angel of the Lord showed his face,

And gazed into the eyes of a cowardly race.

He said, "The judging of you started long ago,

When will it end, only God will know."

When the angel had turned his face and went away,

The race doubted that they saw him, on the same day.

This problem has always plagued man,

Having belief in something, they can't understand.

The road to the Lord is simple and plain,

No understanding is required,

Just, belief in His Name.

TRUST IN HIM

Gaze into the eyes of a lonely man,

His depth is so vast you can't understand.

Once there was a spark of life,

He was a husband, who had a son, and a wife.

That was before that fatal night,

When a stranger came and took their life.

Their end was his end, and its all just pain,

Because, when you treasure humanity,

You treasure, in vain.

Put your faith, not in a son, or a wife.

Evil can come and quickly snuff out their life.

Trust in God, for He is the only light,

That can still keep your son and wife,

Within your sight.

Even after this life,

Has said it's goodnight.

DECEIVER

There was a man known throughout all the land,

And people would come just to shake his hand,

And to listen to the words he spat,

Going over the bible about this and that.

When it was over and they had left,

He would smile his wicked smile.

Knowing that he had fooled them all again,

Then his wife, who was of the same heart,

Said, "Why do they follow you into the dark?"

He said to her, again, and again.

"The foolishness of a man's heart,

He looks for God, where he should not."

LATE BELIEVER

There was once a man who believed there was no God,

So, he did every evil thing that he wanted,

Then one day, he died.

Afterward, he came before the Lord to explain his evilness.

The Lord said, "Why did you not obey my commandments?"

The man said, "I didn't think there was a God or a Heaven,

That's why I was evil.

Now, that I know the truth, send me back,

And I'll be as good as any Christian on Earth.

The Lord said, "Didn't you hear of my Son on Earth?"

"Yes," he said, "But I didn't believe in you,

Surely, I couldn't believe in your Son."

"How did you think you came to be?

If not for my help," asked, The Lord.

"I just didn't believe," said the man.

"But now, I do.

Give me another chance," he said.

"I did, with my Son," said, The Lord.

"Now, just as surely as you know there is a Heaven,

You must also know that there is a Hell,

And as you have met Me, now you shall meet Him."

MAN'S DAMNATION

Man's damnation,

Is our curse.

You can read about it in the bible,

Verse by verse.

The scriptures are nothing,

But the words of time.

As given to mortals,

By the Devine.

We read and we fear,

Still, we refuse to see.

That the Lord, Is the Lord,

And salvation is free.

So, to those, would-be, Christians.

You're right to have fear.

Because the Lord is coming,

And His salvation is clear.

LOOK INTO THE EYES (1)

If you look into my eyes then you could tell,

My soul is scared it's going to hell.

I once said, "I didn't believe in the pie in the sky,

But you'll know the truth if you look into my eyes."

As the years tick by like days,

And death brushes up against your face.

You must believe that there's more to the Earth,

More than just some clay.

Some say that the book is used for mass control,

You know, to keep in line, the young, and the old.

Act nice on Earth or damnation you'll face,

Once you have left the human race.

When I was young, the book was a fright,

Like witches and goblins that lurk in the night,

But now that I'm older, I understand,

It feels like warm gloves,

On cold wintered hands.

LOOK INTO THE EYES (2)

The eyes I told you to look in before,

Were the eyes of a sinner, but I'm a sinner, no more.

With belief comes Courage, Strength, and Faith,

So, when you meet Death, he'll have a friendly face.

For those who fear Death,

Look into their eyes and you'll know.

They're not just scared,

They're scared to the soul.

JUDGMENT DAY

The lightning strikes and the thunder sounds,
And though I was safe, I still looked around.

As a child, I was taught,
Whenever you heard thunder,
It's The Lord's walk.

To the edge of Heaven,
He comes sometimes,
And if He should ever decide,
To come all the way.
Then that will be the judgment day.

So, whenever I hear that thunderous sound,
I know that the Lord is looking down.

Then I quickly drop to my knees and pray,
That this is not the judgment day.

GET USED TO THE BURN

I burned myself on the stove,

And the pain was beyond my control.

It made me think of the eternal burn,

That awaits those who have refused to learn.

That the Lord is King and Master of all,

And the commandments He made,

Are not seasonal.

So, if you refuse them,

Then there's nothing to learn.

All I can say,

Is get used to the burn.

One that's not just a flash of pain,

But an eternal agony,

That will always remain.

NO ONE KNOWS HIS TIME

I heard you were talking about the Lord,
Claiming He was a fraud.

But look at you now,
On your knees trying to pray,
Because it's Judgment Day.

But your time has already come and passed,
And only the righteous ones will last.

This is only a warning, ahead of time,
Get in line with the Devine.

Because the Lord will come,
And pull souls from their graves.

All names will be called,
But not all will be saved.

SIN'S BED

Yes, I can stand the pain,

Even though I'm at the threshold,

Of being driven insane.

I wish it was a simple pain,

The kind that would heal,

Or a timely one,

That I could conceal.

But it's neither and to my dread,

It's mentally working on my head.

The pain I feel is very old,

And it was inherited when I got my soul.

Through generations of space and time,

The pain of the soul was transferred to the mind.

So, to cure the pain that's in your head,

You must first cleanse the soul,

Where sin, has made a bed.

UNSEEN

We see it coming like the seasons,

We even say we understand it,

But we're still afraid, beyond all reasons.

The strongest of men will simply break,

Once served this cold, cold, plate.

When I was a child, he was never in my mind,

Even though he was around me all the time.

Now that my hair is turning gray,

I see his face every day.

He doesn't speak, lust passes me by,

And I don't know the reason why.

Am I closer to the spirit, is that what enables me to see,

Or am I so far away that he comes closer to me?

In a little while I will know,

If he's a friend,

Or a foe.

THE MADNESS

I would stop the madness.

If it was within my grasp.

But it's something that is passed,

From generation to generation, from time to place.

It's why the Egyptians are no longer the dominant race,

When Adam and Eve first took the bite,

The madness arose and took its first flight.

Some call it a gift, some the sight.

Hitler had it, and Judas, but only for a night.

I had the madness deeply embedded in myself,

So, I prayed for forgiveness and the madness left.

It's there in some clear to the bone,

To destroy it, one just needs to atone.

Now, the races are all in trouble again,

But, this time, the madness,

Is coming from within.

46

WANT

A man was traveling in the dark,

And came upon a light in a park.

He looked into the light above,

And it showed him two crowns.

One was him in his homeland,

Being the riches of every man.

The other was of him following the light down a path,

To broke to buy even a single blade of grass.

Then the light in the park,

Started to move away from the dark.

He thought about his home again,

Of being the riches in all his land.

Then he turned, very sharp,

And ran deeper still,

Into the dark.

SIGNS OF THE TIMES

The signs have always been in our faces,
But we know the arrogance of humanity.

Foolish we've been since the beginning of time,
We think with our eyes, and not with our minds.

But as the end of life starts to unfold,
Many will realize what was long ago told.

That those who seek their Heaven on Earth,
Will curse the day of the rapture,
Because its signal's the end,
Mankind's final chapter.

ONLY GOD KNOWS

Another life was taken today,

In a very senseless way.

As hard as I try,

I just can't seem to understand.

How death can take the most innocent of man,

While letting the evil continue to live,

Spreading hate and destruction and all else they give.

If this is a test, then I have failed,

Because from what I have seen,

Satan has prevailed.

There I go,

Questioning the will of God,

Because life on Earth sometimes gets hard.

Forgive me, my Lord,

It was a moment of sorrow.

Because I know you are, my Today, Tonight,

And all my, Tomorrows.

THE SHEPHERD

There was a vicious wolf in the land,

And it terrorized every man.

Just before dusk, it would come out,

And if caught, it would devour you,

Without a doubt.

One day it was out hunting on the land,

And came upon twelve sheep, and one lamb.

They looked at him and noticed him not,

As if he was a speck of dust in the dark.

As he ran towards these sheep in this quiet place,

He saw that the lamb had changed his face.

He wasn't even a lamb at all, but a shepherd,

With a halo above, and around it, flew twelve doves.

The Shepherd said, "Abide you where you should not,

For all of these are of my flock."

With that, the wolf turned a cowardly face,

And ran and left the quiet place.

He said, "It was better to go and look around, For someplace,

Where the shepherd, couldn't be found."

RISE AWAY

How easily we strike,

With the venom of a snake.

We dig down deep,

And bring up hate.

But after that moment of hatred has passed,

Another will come and make us laugh.

But it's just Satan, pulling us on a string,

When we roll down, we're evil,

When we roll up, we sing.

So, whenever you feel,

That touch of hate.

Know that it's Satan,

And rise away from the bait.

FAITH

If you believed, what would it mean?

Would you be able to see something you've never seen?

Could you see Heaven or walk past sin?

These are the questions that baffle man,

And that was the Lord's plan.

Believe what you want and do what you like,

And the Lord will judge, whether it's wrong,

Or it's right.

LOOKING FOR HEAVEN (1)

I traveled through the desert in search of a land,

Where men don't hate their fellow man,

Where the different races of the world have no strife,

And a husband will love only his wife.

Where death is never by a violent hand,

And crime is something they cannot understand.

This place I am told is far away,

And to get there I must travel for many days.

I had traveled so long that I had lost track of time,

And I thought I was also losing my mind.

Here in the desert was the greenest grass,

And the contents of the air had changed that fast.

The sun was no longer a burning fireball,

But was cool to the skin, like in the fall.

Children of all colors played together in the grass,

And I could hear their joyous laughter.

LOOKING FOR HEAVEN (2)

A man came up to me as I fell on my knees,
I could see by his face, that he was well pleased.

He said, "This place is not for all,
I'm glad your soul heard the call."

My body felt light as it could be,
I was wondering what had come over me.

I looked back,
And my body was behind me, lying in the sand,
And I knew this was not a mortal land.

If you would like to find this land that I've found,
Keep yourself, Righteous, Steadfast, and Sound.

KNOWING THE TRUTH

I had a dream late one night,

And in that dream, there was a light.

A voice came from within the light.

It said, "Tell me your heart's all,

And all will be known to you."

I asked, "Why is white, white,

And black, black,

And yellow, yellow,

And red, red."

The voice said, "They are only as they are,

Because you look at them that way.

If you look with your heart, instead of your eyes,

You will see that white is really, black,

And black is really, red, and red is really, yellow.

Then it was all made clear to me,

There was no difference between the colors,

Only the difference my mind put on them.

PRAYER OF ENDURANCE

Lord,

Forgive a son and bless a man,

Now that I finally understand.

Give me the courage to accept my plight,

Give me the knowledge to do what's right.

In the face of sin, make me strong.

On the path of righteousness, lead me on,

Deep into its depths, until I'm lost.

When this night is over and I'm awake,

I know your presents will not dissipate.

Because you've been with me, from the beginning,

And I know you'll be here until the end.

And after this life for me is over,

I know you'll be there again.

www.ingramcontent.com/pod-product-compliance
Lightning Source LLC
Chambersburg PA
CBHW020342130626
46549CB00003B/1256